I LOVE THAT YOU ARE MY

46155878R00061

Made in the USA
Lexington, KY
23 July 2019